I0105512

TIME FOR DELIVERANCE

Addiction Recovery Devotional

PASTOR CARL FLOWERS

Trinity Outreach Publishing

Picayune, MS 39466

Trinity Outreach Publishing
502 Jarrell St
Picayune, MS 39466

Copyright © 2017 by Carl Flowers

All rights reserved. This book is protected under the copyright laws of the United States of America. This book may not be copied or reprinted for commercial gain or profit. The use of short quotations or occasion page happy for personal or Recovery Groups as a text book to recovery is permitted and encouraged. Permission will be granted upon request. Unless otherwise identified, scripture quotations are from the King James Version, the NIV, or Message Versions of the Bible.

Take note that the name satan and related names are not capitalized. We choose not to acknowledge him, even to the point of violating grammatical rules.

For information address Trinity Outreach Publishing Rights Department, 502 Jarrell St, Picayune, MS 39466

First Paperback edition February 2017

Manufactured in the United States of America

ISBN-13: 978-0692843086 (Carl Flowers)
ISBN-10: 0692843086

It is my prayer that this will be made available to Christian bookstores and distributors worldwide.

TABLE OF CONTENTS

Dedication

I would like to dedicate this book to the ARRM - Addiction Recovery Restoration Ministry class participants.

2 Corinthians 5:17 - Therefore if any man be in Christ, he is a new creature: old things are passed away; behold, all things are become new.

I would like to dedicate this deliverance devotional to all those who have struggled or in the midst of struggling with addiction. I prophesied to you allow the Lord to heal you through His Word in your journey and I guarantee that He will deliver you as you study the Word of God to build up your spiritual man.

Visit Trinity Outreach Ministries Bookstore. My books are also available online at Amazon.com, BarnesandNoble.com, and BooksaMillion.com

Apostle Carl Flowers, author of "From Sin & Shame to Glory", "Finish Strong", "Spiritual Kryptonite" and "Time for Deliverance".

Preface

Prophetic Proclamation

Acts 10:38 - How God anointed Jesus of Nazareth with the Holy Ghost and with power: who went about doing good, and healing all that were oppressed of the devil; for God was with him.

I prophesy that the same Jesus who delivered many is about to deliver you. I decree and declare that everything that Satan has oppressed you with is about to leave in Jesus name.

Matthew 7:7-8 - Ask, and it shall be given you; seek, and ye shall find; knock, and it shall be opened unto you: For every one that asketh receiveth; and he that seeketh findeth; and to him that knocketh it shall be opened.

I prophesy to you that doors are about to be opened in your life, and therefore you should walk in total victory. The Spirit of the Lord will give you yourself back, your family back, your marriage back, and even your kids back. You will be able to hold down a good job, you will have healthy relationships, and you will experience total victory in Jesus name.

Isaiah 53:5 - But he was pierced for our transgressions; he was crushed for our iniquities; upon him was the chastisement that brought us peace, and with his wounds we are healed.

The Spirit of the Lord is about to heal you of all the wounds in your life. Everything that has been holding you in bondage in regards to your addiction is about to come up and out and God is about to set you free in Jesus name.

Acts 5:16 - There came also a multitude out of the cities round about unto Jerusalem, bringing sick folks, and them which were vexed with unclean spirits: and they were healed every one.

I prophesy that you are coming out the environment of the addicted and afflicted and your wilderness experience it is about to be over, in Jesus name.

1 John 5:14-15 - And this is the confidence that we have in him, that, if we ask any thing according to his will, he heareth us: And if we know that he

hear us, whatsoever we ask, we know that we have the petitions that we desired of him.

I prophesy that you will perfect your prayer life. Not only will you pray for yourself, you will spend time interceding for others.

Acts 4:29-30 - And now, Lord, behold their threatenings: and grant unto thy servants, that with all boldness they may speak thy word, By stretching forth thine hand to heal; and that signs and wonders may be done by the name of thy holy child Jesus.

I prophesy signs and wonders will happen in your life as you commit to Jesus Christ.

I prophesy that you shall be delivered!!

Chapter One – Acknowledgement

Acknowledgement - Acceptance of the truth or existence of something.

First, you must acknowledge that the addiction exists. Many who are caught in the trap of addiction will deny the problem.

Proverbs 28:13 - He who conceals his transgressions will not prosper, but he who confesses and forsakes them will find compassion.

Often times in my life, I went to the extreme in order to cover up a lie and hide my addictions. Before losing everything, I had to acknowledge my Sin in confess to Jesus Christ as my Lord and Savior.

I went to unheard of extremes while hiding and covering up my addictions. I had to acknowledge that I really had a problem and begin to confess my sin. When l acknowledged my sin, it opened up the door for deliverance.

The Prayer of Deliverance

Psalm 51 - Have mercy upon me, O God, according to thy lovingkindness:

according unto the multitude of thy tender mercies blot out my transgressions.

2 Wash me throughly from mine iniquity, and cleanse me from my sin.

3 For I acknowledge my transgressions: and my sin is ever before me.

4 Against thee, thee only, have I sinned, and done this evil in thy sight: that thou mightest be justified when thou speakest, and be clear when thou judgest.

5 Behold, I was shapen in iniquity; and in sin did my mother conceive me.

6 Behold, thou desirest truth in the inward parts: and in the hidden part thou shalt make me to know wisdom.

7 Purge me with hyssop, and I shall be clean: wash me, and I shall be whiter than snow.

8 Make me to hear joy and gladness; that the bones which thou hast broken may rejoice.

9 Hide thy face from my sins, and blot out all mine iniquities.

10 Create in me a clean heart, O God; and renew a right spirit within me.

¹¹ Cast me not away from thy presence; and take not thy holy spirit from me.
¹² Restore unto me the joy of thy salvation; and uphold me with thy free spirit.
¹³ Then will I teach transgressors thy ways; and sinners shall be converted unto thee.
¹⁴ Deliver me from bloodguiltiness, O God, thou God of my salvation: and my tongue shall sing aloud of thy righteousness.
¹⁵ O Lord, open thou my lips; and my mouth shall shew forth thy praise.
¹⁶ For thou desirest not sacrifice; else would I give it: thou delightest not in burnt offering.
¹⁷ The sacrifices of God are a broken spirit: a broken and a contrite heart, O God, thou wilt not despise.
¹⁸ Do good in thy good pleasure unto Zion: build thou the walls of Jerusalem.
¹⁹ Then shalt thou be pleased with the sacrifices of righteousness, with burnt offering and whole burnt offering: then shall they offer bullocks upon thine altar.

I prayed this prayer many times in my recovery. God will deliver you as well when you pray this prayer and believe God for your total deliverance, acknowledging that you have fallen short from His grace. Allow Him to give you strength through His Word. Devote yourself in your local church, serve faithfully, pray daily, and keep your vows unto the Lord.

Chapter Two – Recognize

Recognize – to identify (someone or something) from having encountered them before; know again.

You must recognize that what you are doing is wrong. Addicts find a way to justify their problem in their mind.

1 John 2:16 - For all that is in the world being the lust of the flesh, and the lust of the eyes, and the boastful pride of life, is not from the Father, but is from the world.

In Chapter One, we learned to acknowledge Jesus through the power of prayer. Now, the Holy Spirit wants you to recognize Him by forming a habit to pray.

Proverbs 3:6 - In all your ways acknowledge him, and he will make straight your paths.

Like David, most Bible believing Christians recognize and accept, at least intellectually, the need and importance of prayer. We read books on prayer, we talk about it, we ask for prayer from time to time, but somehow, the church today is anything but a praying church. We may have a few real prayer warriors, but the DISCIPLINE AND PURPOSE of Biblical praying as committed disciples of the Lord Jesus has somehow escaped the body of Christ. We talk of its necessity, but too often we fail to accomplish its reality. I said that to say this: It is important as Christians, as well as a recovering addicts, that we continue to pray. It is a must that we become prayer warriors.

The disciples had this same experience. They, too, fell short in their prayer life and they felt it deeply. It is one thing when don't pray; it is quite another when we fall short. One of my famous quotes is, "Little prayer, little power; much prayer, much power; little study, little growth". Recognize that your addiction has caused your life to be unmanageable and that you are powerless; especially when you don't pray. You will now walk in victory on your way to being delivered from every addiction.

We had an evil and bad spirit in dealing with our addictions. Now it's time to be delivered.

1 John 4:2 - This is how you can recognize the Spirit of God: Every spirit that acknowledges that Jesus Christ has come in the flesh is from God.

We failed many tests and relapsed back into the same old cycle of despair. Seeing now as we learn how to pray and seek God daily, we will pass the test.

2 Corinthian's 13:5 - Examine yourselves to see whether you are in the faith; test yourselves. Do you not realize that Christ Jesus is in you-- unless, of course, you fail the test?

God wants you to know yourself again. He wants you to know your family, your spouse, and your children. He wants you to be a productive citizen. Now that you are seeking Him for deliverance, yes you can have all these things.

Chapter Three – Take Responsibility

I could not be the man of God I am today if I did not take responsibility for my sins. My addiction was just a byproduct of what I was feeling, which was the major contributing factor along with the spiritual warfare and ignorance, as to what was really going on in my life. When I took full responsibility, God not only restored my soul he restored my marriage and my future. When God delivers you, it will bring success in your family life as well.

When I confessed Jesus Christ as my Lord and Savior, I had made up my mind that I was going to take full responsibility of everything I had done. It wasn't an easy process, but it is by far a whole lot better serving in the Kingdom of God.

In my first book, "From Sin & Shame To Glory", I closed out chapter 5 stating that I had issues with my father for a long season for him not being in my life. I did blame him on occasion, but it was God who deleted the bitterness I was grasping hold of. Things became better in our relationship as the Holy Spirit brought our hearts together.

I would like to share some nuggets with you on taking responsibility when you are in relationship with other people.

You must not blame others. Stop saying and thinking, "If only my wife/husband were just more affectionate", or "If women/men were not so seductive". Adam blamed Eve and she blamed the serpent. Instead, you must begin to take responsibility for your actions.

Importance of Taking Responsibility for an Addiction

In order for people to escape addiction, it is vital that they take full responsibility for their current situation because:

* Nobody can make an addict become sober unless they confine that person to a cell – the addict needs to be a willing participant and take responsibility for their own life. There is the famous saying, "You can take a horse to water but you cannot make it drink."

Psalms 34:17 - The righteous cry, and the LORD heareth, and delivereth them out of all their troubles.

* If the addict does not feel responsible for their recovery, they may do their best to sabotage it.

Galatians 5:1 - Stand fast therefore in the liberty wherewith Christ hath made us free, and be not entangled again with the yoke of bondage.

* In order to build a successful recovery, it will be necessary for the individual to put in a great deal of effort. They will only be willing to commit such effort if they feel responsible for their own sobriety.

* If people do not feel responsible for their own life, it means that they do not believe that their actions will make much difference to their situation. This means that they will not believe that there is any point in trying to become sober.

John 15:7 - If ye abide in me, and my words abide in you, ye shall ask what ye will, and it shall be done unto you.

* Even if the addict manages to become sober they will continue to fall into relapse behaviors

unless they take responsibility for their own life.

Are you blaming God for anything bad that happened to you?

Have you been emotionally wounded in such a way that it is hindering your ability to freely receive love as God intended you to?

Do you have knowledge and revelation of how much God loves you?

Do you have a solid Biblical understanding of how much you are loved with the same kind of love that the Father has for Jesus?

Is there a self-worth issue that makes you feel unworthy to be loved?

Settling these issues lays a foundation for breaking free from the power of addictions. You must repair the damage and faulty thinking which hinders your ability to receive the love that God has for you.

* Nobody else can do the work for the individual in recovery. You have to stick with it.

The only way to Deliverance is the Biblical way.

Matthew 10:1 - And when he had called unto him his twelve disciples, he gave them power against unclean spirits, to cast them out, and to heal all manner of sickness and all manner of disease.

* The action of the addict impacts other people. If the individual does not take responsibility for their actions it will mean that these loved ones will continue to suffer.

* If people fail to take responsibility for their future they will almost have dark days ahead. Nobody gets a free ride in life.

* If people do not feel responsible for their own life, they can be full of anxiety and dissatisfaction. They feel completely powerless and at the whims of fortune.

* When people do not feel responsible for their actions they become willing to do terrible things. Humans are capable of almost anything when they do not feel responsible.

* If the individual does not feel responsible for their situation, they are likely to suffer from a great deal of negativity. This pessimism can suck away any motivation.

It's time for you to be motivated take full responsibility of your actions, God is calling you to total deliverance in every area of your life I prophesy that everything will work out for you in Jesus name .

Chapter Four – Accountability

Accountability - the fact or condition of being accountable; responsibility.

Make yourself accountable to a spiritual authority, perhaps a pastor or mature believer. Everybody needs a "safe" person to share their struggles with.

> *James 5:16 - Therefore, confess your sins to one another and pray for one another, so that you may be healed. The effective prayer of a righteous man can accomplish much.*

Be subject to leadership. It is very important that you get involved in your local church. Often times we put off going to church *because* of our struggles, when in fact, the church is like a spiritual hospital. You need to allow Jesus Christ to be head of our life. You need to pray and ask God to send you to a church that will minister to the needs of you and your family.

This is the most important step in recovery. As soon as you find that place, stay under your leader. God will lead you to your deliverance. It is going to take some work on your part, but be dedicated, remain steadfast, and watch your people places and things and change your environment.

Accountability is so important. At this point, you need to be completely transparent. The Lord will be your leader on exactly what you need at this time, so don't short change yourself. Give it your all, because you have a lot to lose.

Satan wants destroy you in your addiction; but I just want to share with you that this is your season and your time to be delivered. Confess when you have had a bad day. You will have some bad moments, but God will give you the power to overcome.

Accountability will give you confidence; it will give you the courage to move on and pursue what He has called you to do. God is going to heal you of your self-inflicted wounds. God is going to restore you, your marriage, your family, and your future. Get used to being happy, because you deserve everything God has for you.

I just want to continue to encourage you to be accountable to your spiritual leadership, your Sponsor, your AA meetings and 12 step program. Do whatever it takes for you to get your deliverance.

My spiritual father was there for me at a crossroads in my life when I had relapsed on crack cocaine. I will never forget the love that reached out to me. It was God moving in him to help me when I couldn't help myself. That is the importance of an accountability partner. Always keep your heart open, get around people that are going to help you to be better. Don't settle for what the world has to offer you. You might have done with the world say you have done, but you're not all the world says you are.

You will ask God about everything in prayer and supplication.

You will pray and not lose heart.

You will hear God clearly before making any decisions in every area of your life.

Your prayers are meant to be answered.

You will remind God of His promises that He spoke over your life.

Repeat this:

God, I will pray Your Word over my life; I believe Your Word will not come back to you void. My life has purpose and a meaning.

I declare that I will pray anytime and anyplace.

I declare that whatever I ask in the name of Jesus He's going to do it.

I declare that I will not limit how God responds.

I decree and declare that I can tap into the power of God through prayer.

I declare that I have authority and dominion in prayer.

I declare that I will reach a point of prayer that the devil can't locate me.

True prayer will usher me into the presence of God.

I will embrace the power of God through prayer.

I decree that the Word of God will become real in my spirit man.

I decree and declare that no demonic force can stop me from getting into the presence of God.

In Jesus name, today I will walk in total deliverance.

Chapter Five – Your Will vs. God's Will

John 7:17 - If anyone's will is to do God's will, he will know whether the teaching is from God or whether I am speaking on my own authority.

Romans 12:2 - And be not conformed to this world: but be ye transformed by the renewing of your mind, that ye may prove what is that good, and acceptable, and perfect, will of God.

God's will is His Word. When we expose ourselves to do God's will, we tap into the power of the supernatural.

You must recognize that "will power" is not the answer. At a weak moment, your "will" may fail you every time. By admitting that you are in need of God's help, you then have open access to His supernatural intervention in your life. You must yield your will to God's will. That's when He can begin a new work in your life.

The new work that God is doing in you is powerful. We have to continue to work on our deliverance. The Power that will deliver you is doing a new work and your whole family, praise God! Now all that is left to do is daily walk out your confession in the power of God. Jesus said, "If any man should come out to me he must deny himself and take up his cross and follow me."

By now you are ready to walk this thing out ! You are ready to experience the new life. God's will is bringing everything to pass. Ask yourself this question, "How would I continue to deceive myself? How much more can my family take? What is my purpose here on earth? Everything that had you bound has to let you go now in the Power of the Holy Spirit. Every spiritual kryptonite and every lustful appetite, every demonic influence that ever came in your life has to flee when it's time to be delivered. Today, begin speaking the Word over your life.

Decree and declare the Word over your life:

I will not accept any counterfeit anointing over my life.

I break off every demonic confederacy associated with the spirit of seducing.

I sever my ties with any seducing spirit.

I will have no association with a seducing spirit.

I will not be lead down a path of destruction in the name of Jesus.

I declare I will not be seduced into submission.

I declare and decree every stronghold associated with the seducing spirit is broken in Jesus name.

I will not allow the old patterns of addiction defeat me again in Jesus name.

I will not accept any familiar spirits over my life in Jesus name.

I will not get into the environment that reminds me of my addiction in Jesus name.

I confess that I shall be delivered in Jesus name.

I turn my will over to Jesus by my confession of deliverance and I will submit myself to His Word.

I will commit myself to prayer daily in Jesus name.

I will not allow this spirit to undermine and distort my moral and spiritual judgment.

Father God, I cancel the war of lust between spirit and flesh and I cover myself with the blood of Jesus.

I declare that I will not fall under the spirit of adultery in the name of Jesus.

Your word tells me to abstain from fornication.

I will no longer go against God's moral laws.

God I know that I am sanctified and set free.

I will not allow any demon to tell me that pornography is innocent fun.

No longer will I be a slave to any demonic forces in Jesus name.

I will not allow satan to whisper satanic thoughts into my mind.

I will not believe the lies from the pits of hell.

I will not turn back to that which reminds me of my past in Jesus name.

I will not associate with anything or anyone who reminds me of my past in Jesus name.

Chapter Six – Study the Word

James 1:21 - Therefore putting aside all filthiness and all that remains of wickedness, in humility receive the Word implanted, which is able to save your souls.

It is now very important that you not only find a local church, but you also start to become accountable to a spiritual father, as well as attend your recovery meetings. You now know how to put the work in. You now have to put aside all filthiness of your spirit.

Study the Word of God that you will know what to do when you are tempted. Just because you are committed to the Word of God does not mean that you will not encounter tests. Common things will come into your life. People places and things will constantly remind you of your past, but the power of God's Word will keep you focused on your future.

You have it in you to study. Your life is a book and you are now writing the best chapters of your life. God has brought you from sin to victory. Now, all you have to do is to continue to allow that to approve you daily to be faithful at His Word. Finish strong, beloved!

By now you are well on your way in deliverance.

2 Timothy 2:15 - Study to shew thyself approved unto God, a workman that needeth not to be ashamed, rightly dividing the word of truth.

By studying the Word of God confess these words over your life daily:

I decree that the revelation of God has changed my mindset.

I will do the will of God while on earth.

My thought pattern will not pervert the Word of God that inside of me.

I will not think in and old mindset.

I will allow the revelation of God to renew my mind and I will walk it out in Jesus name.

No revelation will stay locked in my mind.

I do not have an unrestrained mindset; I have the mind of Christ in Jesus name.

I will prepare the way for my mind to be renewed.

I will take charge of my life by submitting to the Word of God.

The knowledge of God will transform me.

I will prove how good and effective the Word of God is in my life.

I will not stay stuck under a revelation.

I will watch the Word of God manifest in my life, my church, my region, and my nation.

I will prove the will of God in Jesus name.

I will speak the revelation of God on earth.

I will no longer speak ignorantly of the kingdom of God.

I recognize what time it is.

It is time for me to submit to the Word.

It is time for me to get my life back on track.

It is time for me to love again in Jesus name.

Now is the time for my deliverance.

I will take my studying seriously.

I will not give up, but show up to be the man/woman God called me to be.

I will not turn back and go back to my addiction.

The present truth of God changed my mindset.

The spirit of religion will no longer make the Word of God have no effect in Jesus.

I declare that I am not the focus of my mentality.

I will listen and obey the voice of God.

I have the King and the Kingdom inside of me.

No demonic activity is allowed to operate inside of my mind.

I know that God has cleaned me up and renewed my mind so I can go back and rescue the ones that are stuck in the mess I was in.

I will advance the kingdom of God on earth.

I will stay humble knowing that I have not delivered it myself. It was the power of God that set me free in Jesus name.

Chapter Seven – Don't Hold Onto Stuff

Ecclesiastics 7:18 (AMP) - It is good that you take hold of one thing (righteousness) and also not let go of the other (wisdom); for the one who fears and worships God [with awe-filled reverence] will come forth with both of them.

Acts 19:18-20 - And many that believed came, and confessed, and shewed their deeds. Many of them also which used curious arts brought their books together, and burned them before all men: and they counted the price of them, and found it fifty thousand pieces of silver. So mightily grew the word of God and prevailed.

Often times, people get caught up into their addictions like I did by holding on to stuff. Satan and the demonic spirits will constantly fight you and your deliverance; they won't quit. The Bible tells us to be not ignorant of his devices. Demonic spirits can attach even in a text message or numbers in your phone device. Holding on to phone numbers, pictures of people who you used with, or visiting people and places that you know in your spirit that is not good for you is a major pitfall.

You must destroy all the evidence that was allowed to bring you under spiritual bondage. You must destroy any drug paraphernalia, pornographic websites, and pictures in your possession. You can't wean yourself off pornography or any other addiction if you are trying to hide stuff that you tend to go back to.

Think of the hidden drugs, paraphernalia, or pornography in your home as a ticking time bomb that will ultimately destroy your family and marriage. Even though we get delivered, satan will use the same people, places and things to try to lure you back into your addiction.

I know that we are now reading the Word, studying it, and praying in all the things we need to do; but it is very important that we destroy the evidence. Make sure that you remove all the paraphernalia from out of your possession. Whatever it takes! As I mentioned in the book, 'Spiritual Kryptonite", in Chapter One, our computer websites and technology are awesome, but we are just one click away from being caught back up in our addictions. Don't hold onto stuff; get it out of your possession; get it off your phone, out of your closets and your house. Put the evidence where it belongs – in the garbage. The Spirit of the Lord has delivered us; therefore, there is no reason for us to hold onto the paraphernalia.

Even though you go to church and get in the Word and love Jesus Christ, always keep in mind that your addiction was a major problem and that you could not save yourself. God saved you and delivered you out. The potential of relapse is always there so be aware of your limitations.

Confess this word over your life:

Now that I am delivered, I will not hold onto anything that reminds me of my past. I must say that when I first got delivered, I was caught up in multiple relapses that I did not plan on because I had paraphernalia in my possession. I will safeguard myself by being aware of my weakness. I will not set myself up for failure.

I decree and declare that I will no longer reason with sin.

My heart is fully submitted to God.

I have been drawn away from my own lusts.

Father God, I ask that you fully deliver me from this sexual sin.

I am set free from any and all evil spirits that have attached themselves to me because of my involvement in this activity.

satan you are a liar, murder, and a deceiver in the name of Jesus. I rebuke you satan with the blood of Jesus.

I renounce any involvement with pornography and sexual perversion in the name of Jesus.

I will not hold on to drug paraphernalia in the name of Jesus.

I will not visit explicit websites in the name of Jesus.

No unclean spirit will twist or pervert my thinking in the name of Jesus.

I declare that I will no longer feel emotionally and mentally raped in Jesus name.

I break off every spirit of suicide, death and destruction in Jesus name.

I break every demonic confederation associated with any unclean spirit.

Father God, encamp your guardian angels around my bedpost so no unclean spirit can give me nightmares.

I repent from any and all demonic activities in the name of Jesus.

I will prevail in the Word in Jesus name.

I decree and declare that I am delivered in Jesus name.

I confess the Word of God over my life in Jesus name.

Chapter Eight – Transformation

Transformation - a thorough or dramatic change in form or appearance.

> *2 Corinthians 3:18 - And we all, who with unveiled faces contemplate the Lord's glory, are being transformed into his image with ever-increasing glory, which comes from the Lord, who is the Spirit.*

> *Acts 3:19 - Repent, then, and turn to God, so that your sins may be wiped out, that times of refreshing may come from the Lord.*

After God delivers us from our addictions, we don't even look like what we've been through. The glory of God begins to manifest from the inside out. We begin to take on a new attitude and we possess a new glow. We begin to walk in the glory of the resurrection power of Jesus Christ. Amen!

We don't have to go back to the school of shame. We have been there and done that and have been delivered from it.

We have to constantly believe in ourselves, even if we have had some slip, trips, and falls. I want you to know that you are not perfect; you will make some mistakes in your recovery, even when you do get back up and begin to do what God called you to do. Even now, every moment that I get low, I will encourage myself with prophetic proclamation.

Decree and declare this word over your life:

I declare that I have a spiritual right to forget my past.

I believe the grace of God is sufficient for me.

The storms of my life will activate what God has put inside of me.

I will not let the vision God gave me perish.

I will watch as the Word of God manifests in my life, my family, my church, my region, in my nation.

I will dedicate myself to the purpose in the power of prayer and fasting.

The present truth of God changed my mindset.

The spirit of religion will no longer make the Word of God have no effect in Jesus name.

I will operate as God on earth.

I declare that I am not the focus of my mentality.

I will listen and obey the voice of God.

I have the King and the Kingdom inside of me.

No demonic activity is allowed to operate inside of my mind.

I know that God has cleaned me up and renewed my mind so I can go back with a team to witness and rescue the ones that are stuck in the mess I was in.

I will advance the Kingdom of God on earth.

The heart of God will make me rise into position to walk in total deliverance.

I will commit myself and submit myself to the power of the Holy Spirit into those who are in authority over me.

I will never forget that it was God who brought me out of a horrible pit.

I will tell my testimony of deliverance without shame.

I will remember then a call to repentance.

I will never forget where I came from on the way to where I'm going in Jesus name.

Chapter Nine – Give it Time

2 Corinthians 6:2 - he saith, I have heard thee in a time accepted, and in the day of salvation have I succoured thee: behold, now is the accepted time; behold, now is the day of salvation.

Recovery is not a sprint, it is a marathon. I can remember running a track event back in high school; it was the quarter-mile race. I started out real fast, burning everyone on the track; but when I got three-quarters of the way around the track, I was passed by teammates. Not only was I running out of gas, the bear had jumped on my back, in the cubs were trying to trip me up. About the time I got to the finish line, not only was I losing, but I was also cramped up and downtrodden and burnt out.

From that point on, I learned how to pace myself in that particular race. Learning from my mistakes, I went on to place well in the state competition. It takes discipline and proper training techniques to be all you are going to be. You have to take time to train, to get your proper form, to get in condition to be the best you can be.

Take the time to be coached, accept the correction, and learn from your mistakes. In running the long distance Christian race, you have to pace yourself. Give yourself time to work through the process of recovery. More often than not, God chooses to take us through a learning and growing process that can be very painful. Victory over addiction should be viewed as a marathon, not a sprint.

Give yourself time and take your time to get to know yourself again. Invest in your relationships. We were fine after we've been delivered from our addictions, but now we have to rebuild, rekindle, and fortify our lives.

By now you are discovering that God will not leave you by yourself. You are now learning that it's going to take a consistent effort on your part to maintain your deliverance in the spirit of holiness. God didn't call you to be conformed to the world, He has called you to grow in wisdom. Take time to learn from your mistakes, take time with your family, and take time to rebuild.

It is now time to invest in your future - to redeem the time.

It's deliverance time.

Let honor come to our name.

It's time to be delivered.

Let songs of worship come from our spirits in the name of Jesus

My lips are anointed to sing, my hands are lifted to praise God.

The God in me shall spring forth in the name of Jesus.

My voice shall cancel the assignment of the enemy.

I will not give up or give in.

I'm called to change the nations with my praise.

I command my spirit to reverence the spirit of God.

I decree and declare that warfare is broken off my life when I worship.

There is no limit to my praise.

My worship makes war with every demonic spirit that comes against the Lamb of God.

My emotions are blessed and healed by my praise.

My praise has silenced the voice of darkness away from me.

No devil shall come in my presence in Jesus name.

I confess my deliverance in Jesus name.

Who the Son sets free is free indeed in Jesus name.

Chapter Ten – The Deliverance of Israel

In the book of Exodus, the 14th chapter, it seems as though Israel was taking it one day at a time, trusting and depending on God to move them to their destiny.

It's cliche, but you must approach your addiction one day at a time. Look for little victories and rejoice in the progress you're making. Recovery is a cinch by the inch, but a trial by the mile. The Spirit of the Lord has riches in the lowest valley to bring you over the highest mountain. When it is time for your deliverance, God will go to the extreme to bring you out your bondage.

In the book of Exodus, 14th chapter, Israel is at the Red Sea following the decision of Pharaoh.

The decision of Pharaoh: He regretted his decision to free Israel, then orders the Egyptian army, to include 600 chariots, to capture the Israelites by the Red Sea.

The despair of the people: This decision causes them to want to give up (Exodus 14:10 - 12). In great fear and anger, the Israelites cry out to Moses, "Our Egyptian slavery was far better than dying out here in the wilderness!"

The declaration of Moses: Look up!! (Exodus 14:13-14). Moses reassures them, "Don't be afraid. Just stand here and watch the Lord rescue you." This is what happens when we total surrender to the Lord. He begins to move on our behalf. He will put men and women of God in leadership positions to lead you to your destiny. No matter how many of satan's demonic forces are trying to come up against you, if God be for you it is more in the world than is against you.

The decree of God: Lift up! (Exodus 14:15-18). Moses raises his staff over the Red Sea, dividing the waters, and allows Israel to walk across on dry ground.

I come to tell you that the Spirit of the Lord will call supernatural things to happen in your life. The Spirit of God will rescue you just in the nick of time. God will call you to cross over on dry ground. Israel crosses over the Red Sea.

The protecting: The pillar of cloud moves between the Egyptians in the Israelites (Exodus 14:19-20). At night it comes as a pillar of fire, once again residing in darkness for the Egyptians but the glorious light for the Israelites.

The parting: A strong east wind blows and parts the Red Sea, farming walls or water and each side (Exodus 14:21-22).

The perishing: In an attempt to pursue the Israelites across the dry path, the Egyptians drown when Moses lifts his hand, causing the waters to collapse on them (Exodus 14:23-31). This was an awesome demonstration of the power of God in Moses' life and the lives of the Israelites. The same God who delivered them will also deliver you. Get ready to crossover in your deliverance. Get ready to praise God and worship Him like never before.

The praising: A great victory celebration took place on the hills of the eastern banks of the Red Sea (Exodus 15:1-21). Moses and his sister, Miriam, lead the nation in singing, music, and dancing. Now is the time for you to do your deliverance dance!

I command my praise to agitate demons & devils in the name of Jesus

The enemy will no longer be able to locate me in my praise.

We will sing songs that will produce what God wants in the name of Jesus.

We will create a praise that will brings reverential fear to the kingdom of darkness.

Father God, release an anointing of praise on every musician and release the false musicians in the churches.

Let our praise be blessed to usher us into the presence of God.

I will not give up or give in.

I'm called to change the nations with my praise.

I command my spirit to reverence the spirit of God.

Warfare is broken off my life when I worship.

There is no limit to my praise.

My worship makes war with every demonic spirit that comes against the Lamb if God.

My emotions are blessed and healed by my praise.

My praise has silenced the voice of darkness away from me.

No devil shall come in my presence.

I have access to the throne of God with my worship.

My praise will bring me out and empower me.

I will put on the garment of praise.

I will praise Him for what I came out of.

I will praise Him for what I'm going into.

I will praise and worship Him in spirit and in truth.

Now is the time for my deliverance.

Yes, will I praise Him.

Chapter Eleven – Stay Fit

In this short chapter, it is my intent to point out how important it is to stay in shape, not only physical shape, but mental shape, and most importantly - spiritual shape. Stay committed to be disciplined and dedicated to Jesus Christ. If we truly love Jesus, we will never again turn back to the life we used to live in bondage to sin.

In my second book, "Finish Strong", the Spirit of the Lord allowed me to highlight some important facts in running the Christian race. Again, it is not a sprint, it is a marathon. Just to paraphrase - You will have preliminaries, the semi-finals, and the finals. The first phase is where you make your mistakes. The second phase is where you learn from your mistakes. And, in the third phase, you cross over into victory.

In that particular book I pointed out that we can't be disqualified. Often times we get caught up in the church and we forget about BEING the church. God is so kind to us. We must be fit to walk this race out in faith. He has called us to go the extra mile. He has called us to Finish Strong.

1 Corinthians 9:26-27 - Thus I do not run aimlessly; I do not fight as if I were shadowboxing. No, I drive my body and train it, for fear that, after having preached to others, I myself should be disqualified.

Don't make exercise a half-hearted endeavor! Set goals, create a plan, and then execute it. Don't be afraid to pray for help.

Confess the Word of God over your life daily repeat these declarations out loud repeat it over and over again. Make the Word of God your habit. Get in the practice of confessing. Get in the practice of preventive maintenance. Get in the practice of saying, "Never again!"

Never again will I yield my members as members of unrighteousness, but I yield my members as instruments of righteousness. (Romans 6:13)

Never again will I allow lust to war in my members, causing me to war and fight my brothers and sisters. (James 4:1)

Never again will I allow fornication, uncleanness, inordinate affection, evil concupiscence, and covetousness, which is idolatry, to operate in my members. (Colossians 3:5 KJV)

Never again will I sin against my brethren. (1 Corinthians 8:12)

Never again will I get high off drugs and alcohol.

I will not associate with people who are struggling with an addiction.

I am not strong in myself. In Jesus Christ I confess my strength.

I will live sober. In Jesus name I am delivered.

I am delivered because of my confession.

I am delivered because of my change of heart.

I am delivered because of the blood of Jesus.

I am delivered because Jesus Christ came to set the captives free.

I confess that never again will I battle with the spirit of lust.

I am born again not in porn again.

I am born again so no more of that slipping and dipping in sin again.

I am born again and I will not mourn again for the same old sin.

I will walk out my deliverance one day at a time and give God the glory for my true deliverance.

Chapter Twelve – Our Deliverance

Romans 10:9-11 - That if thou shalt confess with thy mouth the Lord Jesus, and shalt believe in thine heart that God hath raised him from the dead, thou shalt be saved. For with the heart man believeth unto righteousness; and with the mouth confession is made unto salvation. For the scripture saith, Whosoever believeth on him shall not be ashamed.

The Deliverance Story of Jesus Christ

Isaiah 53 - Who hath believed our report? and to whom is the arm of the LORD revealed? For he shall grow up before him as a tender plant, and as a root out of a dry ground: he hath no form nor comeliness; and when we shall see him, there is no beauty that we should desire him. He is despised and rejected of men; a man of sorrows, and acquainted with grief: and we hid as it were our faces from him; he was despised, and we esteemed him not. Surely he hath borne our griefs, and carried our sorrows: yet we did esteem him stricken, smitten of God, and afflicted. But he was wounded for our transgressions, he was bruised for our iniquities: the chastisement of our peace was upon him; and with his stripes we are healed. All we like sheep have gone astray; we have turned every one to his own way; and the LORD hath laid on him the iniquity of us all. He was oppressed, and he was afflicted, yet he opened not his mouth: he is brought as a lamb to the slaughter, and as a sheep before her shearers is dumb, so he openeth not his mouth. He was taken from prison and from judgment: and who shall declare his generation? for he was cut off out of the land of the living: for the transgression of my people was he stricken. And he made his grave with the wicked, and with the rich in his death; because he had done no violence, neither was any deceit in his mouth. Yet it pleased the LORD to bruise him;

he hath put him to grief: when thou shalt make his soul an offering for sin, he shall see his seed, he shall prolong his days, and the pleasure of the LORD shall prosper in his hand. He shall see of the travail of his soul, and shall be satisfied: by his knowledge shall my righteous servant justify many; for he shall bear their iniquities. Therefore will I divide him a portion with the great, and he shall divide the spoil with the strong; because he hath poured out his soul unto death: and he was numbered with the transgressors; and he bare the sin of many, and made intercession for the transgressors.

Hebrews 7:25 - Wherefore he is able also to save them to the uttermost that come unto God by him, seeing he ever liveth to make intercession for them.

My Life Story

After multiple addictions, relapses, agony, and defeat I am delivered in Jesus name.

In troubleshooting my life with addictions, I discovered the root of all my life struggles. My addiction didn't start the first time I drank alcohol or indulged in drugs or even had sex, it all stemmed from the root of Sin. It was that shame that held me in the midst of trying to adapt to my life in attempting healthy relationships with people and with Jesus Christ. After the roller coaster rides of failure and disappointment, not only was I in a crisis, but America was also in a crisis. Our culture was in poverty and at war. Families were migrating from the south to the north to escape the stronghold of racism and poverty. They were looking for hope for a better future for their families, only to discover that no matter where you move, there will still be trouble unless you have Christ in your heart. Only God can bring us from sin and shame to glory.

The glory of God can restore and deliver us out of any crisis of addiction.

Prayerfully, and under the inspiration of the Holy Spirit, I have written this book as a tool of recovery. It is my prayer that you, too, will discover the who, what, when, where, and why of ACTION. Most importantly, the glory of a fully submitted life with Jesus Christ. To God be the Glory!!

I am redeemed from destruction, and I am crowned!

I am delivered in Jesus name and with loving-kindness and tender mercies (Psalm 103:4).

I am delivered in Jesus name.

I am redeemed from all curses of the Law.

I am delivered in Jesus name.

I am redeemed from the curse of poverty.

I am delivered in Jesus name.

I am redeemed from all curses of sickness and disease.

I am delivered in Jesus name.

I am redeemed from all curses of insanity and madness.

I am delivered in Jesus name.

I am redeemed from all curses of fear and terror.

I am delivered in Jesus name.

I am redeemed from all curses of pride and rebellion.

I am delivered in Jesus name.

I am redeemed from all curses of schizophrenia (double-mindedness).

I am delivered in Jesus name.

I am redeemed from all curses of rejection and abuse.

I am delivered in Jesus name.

I am redeemed from all curses of family destruction. I am delivered in Jesus name.

I am redeemed from all curses of witchcraft and idolatry.

I am delivered in Jesus name.

Yes! You are! Yes, you can! Yes, you will stay delivered in Jesus name!!

To God be the glory!!

Dedication

I would like to dedicate this book to the Addiction Restoration Recovery Ministries under the umbrella of the Oasis Community Development Center (ARRM).

I would like to dedicate this deliverance devotional book to all the participants there as mentor and director and founder of this program.

Always remember: You may have done with the world says that you have done; but you are not all the world says you are.

2 Corinthian's 5:17 - Therefore if any man be in Christ, he is a new creature: old things are passed away; behold, all things are become new.

As you know, I walked a mile in your shoes. We are all our work in progress. Now you, too, can walk in victory. Continue to trust God, and whatever you do don't give up. It is time for deliverance. Who the Son sets free is free indeed.

Sinner's Prayer

Father God, in the name of Jesus, I repent from all my sins and invite you into my heart & life as my personal Savior. I believe that Jesus died on the cross for my sins. Please forgive me of the sins I have committed. Right now I confess Jesus as the Lord of my soul. This very moment I accept Jesus Christ as my own personal Savior and according to His Word, right now I am saved.

Therefore, Lord Jesus, transform my life so that I may bring glory and honor to you alone and not to myself. Thank you, Jesus, for dying for me and giving me eternal life.

Your word says in

Romans 10:9 - That if thou shalt confess with thy mouth the Lord Jesus, and shalt believe in thine heart that God hath raised him from the dead, thou shalt be saved.

About the Author

Apostle Carl Flowers is passionate about deliverance Ministry and addiction recovery and gives all the glory to God for his personal deliverance.

Has been in ministry since 1995. He is an ordained Apostle and Licensed Senior Pastor through Trinity Outreach Ministries, and his vision for ministry is to provide life-changing experiences through anointed teaching and preaching of The Gospel of Christ, and by developing and sharing ways for God's people to "live out our faith" in practical yet meaningful ways in our city, our nation, and around the world.

His philosophy is simple. "True Christians follow Christ, relate honestly to God, and make a positive impact everywhere we go"! He hopes that you will come and visit us, and consider becoming a part of our growing ministry.

Our Co-Pastor, Prophetess Julie Flowers, a true Woman of God who is passionate about the true meaning of real salvation. She is a woman of God who preaches and teaches the unadulterated word of truth. Prophetess Julie, Co-Pastor, wants everyone to learn, know, and understand that Salvation is a process that ultimately leads to an Anointing of The Baptism of The Holy Spirit.

She and Apostle Flowers and our entire congregation believe that "signs and wonders" are to accompany the true believers of God's Word, and that there is Peace, Purpose, and Power in living a life that is fully surrendered to The Father, The Son, and The Holy Spirit.

"For Thine is The Kingdom, The Power, and The Glory...forever. This ministry was founded on faith love and commitment. Deliverance healing and restoration has been the children's bread.

Pastor Flowers has a Bachelor degree in Biblical Studies/Biblical Counseling from Covenant Bible College & Seminary in Tallahassee Florida

He is also Author of three other books:

"From Sin & Shame to Glory", "Finish Strong", and "Spiritual Kryptonite".

He is the Founder Director of "Addiction Recovery Restoration Ministry" (ARRM) which teaches weekly the divine word of deliverance through Jesus Christ.

www.ingramcontent.com/pod-product-compliance
Lightning Source LLC
Chambersburg PA
CBHW060621070426
42447CB00040B/2209

9 780692 843086